Rowing Slow

The Secret For Going Fast And Getting What You Want From Your Rowing

2nd edition

Mike Davenport, Ed.D.

© 2019 SportWork, Michael L. Davenport, Ed.D
- All rights reserved
ISBN 9781088509456

No part of this publication may be reproduced or distributed in any form without express permission of the author.

Disclaimer

This workbook is designed to provide information in regard to the subject of rowing equipment. It suggests many actions to take for proper care and use of rowing equipment; however, these actions are not and cannot be exhaustive of all necessary actions.

It is not the intent of this workbook to provide all the information that is available concerning rowing equipment. Every effort has been made to make this workbook as complete and as accurate as possible. However, there may be mistakes, both typographical and in content. Do not rely solely on this product for guidance.

The authors, advisors, and publisher shall have neither liability nor responsibility to any person or entity with respect to any loss or damage caused or alleged to be caused directly or indirectly by the information contained in this report.

The authors, advisors, and publisher shall have neither liability nor responsibility to any person or entity with respect to any loss or damage caused or alleged to be caused directly or indirectly by the information contained in this report.

Table of Contents

About Me ---5

Slow Is Not A Dirty Word ------------------------------------9

A Slow Rowing Start ---17

    Mysteries of Enjoyment ----------------------------------23

A Little Rowing History ------------------------------------33

Today Rowing Is--41

    What's A Rower? --43

Why Do You Row? ---49

    JOB 1: Why Do You Row? --------------------------------52

Do You Enjoy Rowing? ---------------------------------------61

    JOB 2: How Much Enjoyment Are You Getting From Your Rowing? ---62

Is Rowing Right for You? -----------------------------------65

    JOB 3: Is Rowing Right For You? ------------------------66

Now Go Slow --71

About Me

I graduated from Florida Institute of Technology in 1978, and had a very joyful time rowing. After graduation, I was an assistant coach there and spent years coaching rowers and keeping our equipment thriving (which in brackish water is tricky business).

Then off to another 32 years of coaching, at University of Central Florida and as head coach at the University at Albany and Washington College.

Early in those years I saw the challenges that coaches and rowers were having with the rowing equipment. It was then, thanks to the influence of my own stress and overwhelm that I wrote *Nuts and Bolts Guide to Rigging*.

That led to being boatman for the U.S. National Rowing Team from 1992-95, including U.S. World Championship teams during that time, and the 1996 U.S. Olympic Team in Atlanta, GA. Since then I have authored several books and a wealth of articles on coaching, rigging, and rowing, and have spoken regularly at coaching conferences, workshops, and conventions across the country.

I live in Maryland with my family and continue to coach, teach, and help rowers and other coaches succeed. If you'd like more help with your rowing, or coaching (or just want to connect) please try me at either of my two websites:

Rowing Equipment >>> MaxRigging.com
Coaching Sports >>> CoachingSportsToday.com

Or send me an email directly at mike@maxrigging.com

- Rowing Workbooks -

✦ *Buy It Right: 8 Steps to Buy the Rowing Equipment You Need At a Price You Can Afford* (rowing workbook #1)

✦ *Get Ready Now: 12 Immediate Actions to Take Before Your Next Rowing Season* (rowing workbook #2)

✦ *Make It Last Forever: 13 Steps to Help Your Rowing Equipment Last an Eternity* (rowing workbook #3)

✦ *Nuts and Bolts Guide to Rigging: One Hundred and Fifty Steps to help you get the most from the rigging of your rowing equipment*

- Coaching workbooks -

✦ *The 3 Sinister Truths of Coaching Sports Today: And What You Can Do About Them* (coaching workbook #1)

✦ *Build Your Team: How to Create, Develop and Lead The Team of Your Dreams* (coaching workbook #2)   _____

(all these books can be found at Amazon)

Slow Is Not A Dirty Word

What you are about to read is the result of over 40 years of pursing speed. It includes years of thinking about rowing, living rowing, and living with a rower. The concepts and advice that follow are unique, and may be radically different than many of the current and common perceptions in today's rowing world.

That's okay . . . it is a big sport, with plenty of room for different thinking.

Rowing Slow is certainly different thinking.

We move incredibly fast in our world today. And our rowing world is no different. Today we can:

- know the speed of every stroke, updated 3 times per stroke
- analyze the exact time, distance, and course of every piece
- set our rest-time to be parceled out to the exact second
- have race results reported around the world in real-time as they happen

We can put watches on our oars, can connect to satellites to get our speeds, and our coaches can be in the boat with us by remote sensing to their launches.

We have to be at the starting line no later than 2 minutes before race time to have 30 seconds in a race to have an equipment disaster and then have race winners determined by milliseconds.

Time is a huge part of our sport. Speed is even bigger—it is what we live and breathe.

That is fine. *Rowing Slow* is not about trying to change that.

Instead it is about **non-hurry rowing**. It is about enjoying and having an appreciation. It is about finding what is good in our sport, and happiness. **It is about going slow so you can go fast.**

Going fast is great. Yet there is a time to go fast (and to search for speed).

But there must be a place and a time to stop accelerating and actually slow down, or like a meteor entering the Earth's atmosphere you will burn up.

Why You Need This Workbook

This workbook is about getting what you want from your rowing. Rowing slow will get you there.

Rowers in search of speed (and that describes most rowers) move so fast, do so much so quickly, do so many things that they often miss what they are after. Like the outfielder who sprints to catch the fly ball, only to overshoot his mark, often rowers miss something by going fast.

Rowing Slow is about picking the times that you need to go fast, to have the ability to go fast when you need it and slow when it is called for. <u>And going slow is called for.</u>

Too often rowers are crushed by the sheer demands of finding speed. Harangued and pressured to do more and more, go so hard, so intense, that they often find themselves in a constant state of velocity. Add that to a life that is now filled with:

- Blogs, Twitters, Slacks, and an amazing amount of computer apps that are all about doing things faster
- Facebook, Instagram, SnapChat and thousands of social sites
- Smart phones that keep you connected to every aspect of the world
- Cars that talk, tell you where to go, and when you will get there
- GPS, DVR, and non-stop interruptions

It is no wonder that rowers and people can collapse under the constant state of hurry we are in.

> *It seems to me that we are moving towards an historical turning point. For at least 150 years everything has been getting faster – and for the most part speed was doing us more good than harm in that time. But in recent years we've entered the phase of diminishing returns. Today we are addicted to speed, to cramming more and more into every minute. Every moment of the day feels like a race against the clock, a dash to a finish line that we never seem to reach. This roadrunner culture is taking a toll on everything from our health, diet and work to our communities, relationships and the environment.*
>
> \-   Carl Honore', Author, *In Praise of Slow*

And you? Let me ask you this, when is the last time you took a leisurely row? You know, a row that wasn't about speed, didn't concern going faster, wasn't focused on splits and paces and ratings. Just a row.

Heck, when is the last time you just did anything slow?

***Slow* is not a dirty word.**

One thing that might compound this issue is that compared to most organized sports today rowers often get involved in rowing in a backwards manner. Whereas most athletes began playing their sport as a child, a majority of rowers do not start rowing until college—and many more don't pick it up until their late 20s, 30s, or even further along in life.

Often it seems those rowers are in a hurry to catch up with the athletes of other sports who have done their sport for most of their lives. What I've learned is that with some basic tools and understandings many rowers can excel at the sport and find an enjoyment level within their rowing that they never thought possible, regardless of when they started. Some may, in fact, grow to love it.

A critical component of this is going slow.

It is my goal with *Rowing Slow* to help open your eyes and expand your mind not only to the **possibilities of rowing**, but to the **possibilities of your rowing**. And with simple time-proven steps help you find enjoyment from the activity we know as rowing.

Part of those steps is a **Slow** approach to rowing.

The word *Slow* may make you think of lazy, or inept, or non-caring. Or maybe you remember some book you read or heard about years ago (*Zen and the Art of Motorcycle Maintenance* perhaps). Or maybe slow brings the thought of long meditation sessions to mind.

I view the state of **Slow** simply as **a mindful approach to what is happening around you**. It is a way to gain enlightenment (and happiness) through thinking, self-contemplation, and intuition. It is using the ability to stop, process, and then proceed in a non-accelerated manner.

What is great about this slow mindset is that while the effort can be minimal—the rewards can often be huge.

This workbook will show you numerous simple steps you can take, now, to help you get the most from rowing. If you have been hitting your head against the boathouse wall wondering what is going on with your rowing—this could help. If all is well this effort could make it even better. And if your goal is to go as fast as possible, then slowing down might just help you get there sooner.

So, get ready to question, to think, to ponder, to slow down—and to have fun. Mostly though get ready to get the most from your rowing.

(And for you that were Speed Reading this, there is help for you too.)

Here is to your rowing success, as slow or as fast as you want it to be.

Mike Davenport

and two others. We ran over to the tree, flapped our arms, made faces, and yelled, all the while the Director was yelling at his assistant about how much money he was wasting. Finally, we must have looked ferocious enough (or foolish enough) and all the crows left.

The shooting started again and just as the eights started to row a train came across a railroad bridge right behind us. This really pushed the Director over the edge and in frustration he began kicking his chair. The assistant, fearing for his job, and probably his life, went running off after the speeding train.

As quickly as the train appeared it was gone, the shooting resumed, and I forgot all about the Assistant Director. Until about two hours later when he dragged himself back from his chase. He was exhausted, sweaty, covered with dirt, and looked like he had been hit by a bus.

I stared. He caught his breath and finally looked up at me. Told me he had chased the train for quite some time.

I was just about to ask how he could stand such a terrible job with such an ungrateful boss (and also what he was going to do if he actually caught the train) when he began to tell me how he was done. Wanted to do something else. But couldn't leave. The job paid too well. His career in advertising depended on him nailing this job.

I was blown away, and confused. How could someone take so much hassle for a career that seemed to me to be filled with more and more hassles. All the while moving at the speed of . . .well the speed of film.

So, let's turn the focus to you for a moment. **Have you found enjoyment in your rowing and are you happy with it?** When you row do you get pleasure and satisfaction, or are you hassled, crushed, and dragging like our commercial friend? Is rowing a drain on your life's battery "life's battery" or does it recharge it?

Heck, when is the last time you just stopped to get your breath?

I am a firm believer that everyone can and should find enjoyment and happiness when they row. At some level **it is there, it just has to be found.** And to find it you may just have to go slow —not ALL the time, but SOME of the time.

Enjoyment is important—especially in sports. But often it is missing. Here's is a great example of what I mean.

Recent studies show that upwards of 75% of kids who are 13 years-old and under leave organized sports.

And when researchers asked those kids why they quit, the #1 reason they got was, " <u>It was no fun</u>." They did not have time to enjoy what they were doing. They were miserable, and so they left.

Here is something that I want to share with you: finding enjoyment and happiness is not that difficult. They just appear difficult to find because we don't focus on them in our rowing, or in our daily lives. Nor do we hardly ever talk about them. And as a matter of fact the topics of fun, enjoyment, and happiness are rather hush-hush and surrounded by mystery. Most people are moving so fast that they blow right by these important points.

Let's take a look at a couple of the mysteries that are floating around about enjoyment and happiness and see if we can get a few things out in the open.

Mysteries of Enjoyment

Mystery #1: Happiness Is Not Important

I guess this all depends on your viewpoint. If you feel that your purpose in life is to conquer the world, win the most toys and become master of time, space, and the Universe, all the while moving at the speed of light then I guess this thought may be true. But that's not what most people are looking for.

Most folks want four basic things out of life. They want:

- To be productive
- To be liked
- To achieve some notoriety
- To have happiness (and have some enjoyment and fun)

So, you see, happiness is important. It is on almost everyone's **Top Four List**. And as that old, famous baby doctor and pretty-cool rower Dr. Benjamin Spock said, "Happiness is mostly a by-product of doing what makes us feel fulfilled."

Mystery #2: Fun Is A Distraction From Getting Things Done

When I start talking about **fun** I know some people view it as a thief. That whenever *they* enjoy something the act of enjoyment takes away from what they are trying to do. Here's an example…

Each year we hold goal-setting sessions for our rowing team. One year I was lucky enough to have a team of very talented individuals, but they were neither very strong nor very large.

They were going to race people all year who were bigger and much than they were. However, they were determined to be fast.

In one goal-setting session, I mentioned one of the team's goals should be for them to enjoy the season. I wanted them to get to the end of their races and be able to look back and realize that they had had fun and got pleasure and satisfaction from their efforts. To enjoy the journey. I didn't want them to judge their season on their win-loss record only.

This did not sit well with them. Not at all. In fact, several were quite uneasy. "We aren't going to do things for the sake of enjoyment are we?" "Will having fun get in the way of our boat-speed?" they asked.

I realized at that moment that I was surrounded by people who viewed enjoyment as a distraction. I took it as a personal challenge and made it my goal to focus on enjoyment all year long. And to be honest I must say we had one of our best years of racing, and also one of our most enjoyable. Enjoyment did not get in the way, in fact it made us faster.

Mystery #3: If You Enjoy Something, You Are Doing It Wrong

Human beings are very creative; that is one of our high points. One of the interesting things about being a Homo-Sapiens is that if ten of us look at the exact same item, we may very well end up with ten different opinions or descriptions of the exact same thing.

For example, what may be an exciting, comfortable, brand-new, luxury automobile to one fellow may be an environment-destroying, noise-making, moving bio-hazard to another.

This makes life entertaining.

When we are presented with a problem, this creativity lets us look at it and find different ways to solve it. And when we solve a problem in such a manner we tend to enjoy it.

When you are doing something and you are enjoying it, that doesn't mean you are doing it incorrectly; it means that you are doing it the way *you* need to do it. As long as you achieve the results needed, and don't mess up too badly (like blow up the chemistry lab), then you *should* enjoy it.

Mystery #4: My Enjoyment Is Someone Else's Responsibility

Sure.

Just like it is someone else's duty to:
- put gas in your car
- do your laundry
- finish your homework
- increase the size of your bank account
- feed your cat
- go to work for you tomorrow morning

See the trend?

The responsibility for finding enjoyment and happiness rests squarely on your shoulders—no one else's. Don't wait for someone to show you how to enjoy things, those days ended when you graduated from kindergarten.

On a day-to-day basis we accept responsibility for many things, but often not the quality of our life. **We (you and I) need to accept responsibility for how much happiness, enjoyment, and fun we have.**

I'll be real blunt here—if you are not finding enjoyment in what you are doing (work, play, relationships, rowing, etc.), then you are not taking your responsibility to yourself seriously enough. I am not saying that everything is your fault; what I am saying is that it is *your* responsibility—not your boss's, not your teammate's, not your friend's.

Mystery #5: You Should Feel Guilty If You Enjoy Something

There are many things that we do we enjoy. But often we listen to other people and adjust our enjoyment off of their opinions.

How many times have you heard things like, "Ohh…you're not going to actually wear THAT out tonight are you?" Or, "Hmm…that's a nice color car, I guess they didn't have any other color, huh?"

If you enjoy a purple car with big pink polka-dots on it—then enjoy it. If you like wearing Hawaiian shirts to formal parties, then why not?

If you don't conform to other people's ideas of what is right, correct, and proper, then don't worry. It is your right to look at things differently. Guilt should not enter the picture. There is already enough guilt, blame, and self-condemnation in the Universe to go around. Don't add to it by having guilty feelings for what you enjoy.

CLARIFICATION–I am talking about enjoying things within acceptable standards. This means that you are not causing harm to someone else physically, mentally, financially, or socially when you are enjoying something (and you ain't breaking the law).

The act of placing an oar in an oarlock and taking a stroke means you have accepted the responsibility for finding enjoyment when you row and being happy with the results. If you are reading this and:

- Thinking, "Hey, wait a minute. I don't enjoy rowing," not to worry.
- If the thought of the next rowing practice is stressing you out, be mellow.
- If you think you might not be able to row one more stroke, take a deep breath. No need to get tense.

The *Rowing Slow* mindset can help you find enjoyment and happiness. It can send you in the right direction.

This workbook was written with one purpose in mind, to help you learn *how to get* more from your rowing. And when I write "**How To**," I mean **HOW TO**. I'm not going to just zing a bunch of theories at you. Instead, I'm here to act as your guide. Step by step. Lead you down the JOB.

Slowly.

In many chapters I've included a "JOB". A **JOB** is a specific solution to a common problem and will include actions and recommendations for you to take.

Some actions are simple, and actually are just reminders of common sense things that you already know, but might be too distracted or overwhelmed to remember—or do. Other actions will be more advanced.

So this workbook is laid out like this:

Step >>> JOB >>> Action(s)

With these JOBs, some practice, and a little bit of common sense thrown in, you can handle just about anything that comes your way.

One thing before we continue—this workbook is not written just for people who have rowed a million strokes. It is written for the non-competitor, the open-water rower, the disabled rower and the newbies who have just begun their venture into rowing, also.

Okay, enough of the chit-chat. Time to get moving. Take a deep breath, get yourself comfortable, and let's go slow and find some happiness and enjoyment…

A Little Rowing History

Many consider rowing to be the effort of propelling a boat by oars. Sounds simple enough, but that definition doesn't quite cover it.

Rowing is more than just *pulling* or *pushing* on an oar. It involves actions like scheduling, planning, training, repairing, buying, transporting and bargaining.

Disagree?

Try rowing for a while without doing any of these things—especially the bargaining part which tends to be done by rowers looking to get out of household chores when the water is flat and the weather is warm. Oh yeah, rowing is also looking. Looking?

Ah…come on man, did you say *looking*? Yup…*looking*!

I believe that rowing is not merely an activity in your life. Rowing is a reflection of the way we **look** at life. So that's where the *looking* part comes in—rowing is a way of looking at our lives.

What Is The "Act Of Rowing"?

Okay, I just said rowing is more than the physical act of pulling on an oar. Stirring up the waters even more, I'm going to stick my neck *waaaay* out here and tell you winning a race is more than moving a boat faster than other people. (Welcome to the most difficult part of this book to write.)

A little history might be helpful, so why don't we take a look at how it all started…

* * * * *

Way back when, in the ancient days, rowing was used as a method of transportation. When there was water that needed to be crossed, our ancestors would find something that would float, hop on it, and start paddling away with their hands.

One day one of our more clever relatives, a caveman by the name of Budd, came home to dinner…

"Dear, how was your day," his wife asked.

"Terrible," Budd replied. "Get chased by Tyrannosaurs all day. Then get chased by his dog—Tyrannosaurus Rex. Come to river, cross it on log. Move log with hands. Many piranhas…bite, bite, bite. Need band aids."

"Ah…poor Budd, here are your band aids. Now there seems to be a simple solution to your dilemma. Why don't you go into basement and invent something to move the log safely. An extension of your arms will help you propel it. Something to keep your hands out of the water so the piranhas won't bite you."

"Smart wife! Me do that now. One question. What is basement?"

So, paddles were on their way. And for eons the system of propelling logs by paddles went along fairly smoothly until one day a caveman, by the name of Ca, came home after a particularly hard day at work…

"Dear, how was your day," his wife asked.

"Awful," Ca replied. "Hunt Mammoth all day. Get wool all over me. Then cross river on log. Move it with new paddle—ultra light version called *Budd-light*. Log roll over, me fall in water. Many alligators…bite, bite, bite. Need band aids."

"Ah…poor Ca. Now there seems to be a simple solution to your dilemma Ca. Why don't you go into the garage and invent something more stable than the log. A small displacement vessel, for example, with a low center of gravity. Something that won't roll over, and then the alligators can't bite you."

"Smart wife! Me do that now. One question. What is garage?"

So, boats were on their way. The system of moving boats by paddles went along fairly smoothly until one day an Italian, by the name of Ro, came home after a particularly hard day at work…

"Dear, how was your day," his wife asked.

"Horrible," Ro replied. "Fight Barbarians all day. Then cross ocean in most recent version of Ca boat—called *Ca-New*. Move it with paddle. Paddle is hard work. Get tired. Go asleep in boat. Me fall overboard. Many sharks…bite, bite, bite. Need band aids."

"Ah…poor Ro. Now there seems to be a simple solution to your dilemma Ro. Why don't you go into the workroom and invent something more efficient than the paddle. Possibly a lever that could attach to the boat to increase the leverage and therefore enhance the propulsion. Something so you won't get so tired and therefore won't fall asleep."

"Smart wife! Me do that now. One question. What is workroom?"

Ro invented his new system—called Ro-ing—which used an oar and a rigger. And it became so popular that a whole culture was named in Ro's honor—yes, the Ro-mans!

When people started using Ro's new-fangled system, they found they were more efficient than those folks using paddles. But Ro's system wasn't perfect.

Humans had to sit in a pretty awkward position when rowing— backwards. Because they couldn't see where they were going a few problems popped up— bumping into each other, rowing off the edge of the world—you know, the sort of things that take some of the enjoyment out of your day.

However, besides those few bumps and crashes, things in the rowing world weren't really too bad. That is until—and, if this were a movie this would be the scary music would pipe in—HUMANS DECIDED THEY WANTED TO GO FAST AND RACE EACH OTHER!

"Dear, how was your day."

"Frightful. Me fish all day. Then row hard to get catch to market before other fisherman. Tough to stay competitive. Government officials visit today. Many tax men…bite, bite, bite. Need more money."

"Ah, there seems to be a simple solution to your dilemma. Why don't you go to the local recreational hall and invent something to earn more money. Possibly an event in which you compete with other fisherman to get from point A to point B the fastest. First one there wins a prize put up by sponsor. This way you can earn more money."

"Smart wife! Me do that now. One question…"

"Yes, yes, I know. What is a recreational hall?"

"No, me know that. What is this point A and point B thing?"

So regattas were on their way. More and more of these regattas began, and more and more people competed for more and more prizes. Things got pretty tense and uptight in the rowing world as coaches and rowers started to push harder and harder for speed.

Rowing started to attract a lot of attention, making the papers, becoming a betting man's sport. Then suddenly…whammo…it was all over.

At the turn of the nineteenth century one of the best things to ever happen to rowing took place—**rowing began to lose its popularity as a professional sport**. People stopped betting on it; it lost a lot of its sponsorship, and many people lost interest in rowing.

And this was good! Why?

Because up to that time rowing was not really an enjoyable activity. People had rowed to move themselves around from place to place, as a means of work, or so people could bet on them. Not exactly enjoyable stuff. (Okay, I know there was some college rowing going on, but come on now—you had to grease your pants and slide back and forth on the wood—that's not my idea of enjoyment.)

Nowadays though, things are different, and better. Because people now row for enjoyment—at least that is what they <u>should</u> be doing.

"Dear, how was your day.

"Miserable. I work hard all day, running the largest corporation in the world is a strain—downsizing, layoffs, government regulations, a fluctuating stock market. Very little enjoyment."

"Ah, there seems to be a simple solution to your dilemma. Why don't you join the local rowing club. Then after work you can go to the club and get out and row. I bet you will find that will help you enjoy your life."

"Smart husband! I'll do that now."

Today Rowing Is

That's a brief fabled history of rowing—at least my warped view of it. As you can see, rowing has gone through quite an evolution to get where it is today. Which begs the question, "Well, where exactly is rowing today?"

A good question, if I do say so myself. (And I do.)

Rowing today is unlike what it has ever been. It is becoming more popular than it ever was, with more people rowing now than ever (especially in the case of rowers over thirty-years old).

Rowing is also becoming accepted into our culture more than ever—just look at the movies and commercials where rowing is appearing. The most interesting thing about rowing today is that it is being done for enjoyment, which until recently it never really was.

Rowing offers something for everyone. There are ups and downs, successes and failures, good times and bad. Besides the highs and lows, the activity of rowing is so varied that it has the potential to satisfy almost any person's value.

When I sat down to try to get—really get—a handle on exactly where rowing is today, it became apparent to me that I was going to have a difficult time trying to define what a rower is today.

Well, with all that said, you probably think I'm about to say something bizarre like a rower is not just someone who pulls on an oar (this may scare you, but now you are starting to think like I do!)

What's A Rower?

There is no doubt that a rower is the person in the shell trying to move it along, but this is only one **type** of rower. There are several other types of rowers like:

- the person in the coxswain seat (if there is one)

- the person in the coaching launch (if there is one)

- the person at the boathouse who works on the equipment

- the person at home (be that a parent or significant other) who makes rowing possible

See what I mean. These are all rowers because they are all involved in the activity (granted, at different levels) and they all are affected by it and they also have an impact on it.

To help clarify things somewhat let's try to look at it this way: Today's rowing is actually getting so large that there are now four distinctly different types of rowers. Those types are:

• **Leisure Rower**—someone who rows for health benefits, both mentally and/or physically.

- **Sport Rower**—someone who rows to be competitive with others (i.e. rowers, coaches, and coxswains of a variety of ages, skill levels, and abilities).

- **Livelihood Rower**—someone who earns a living from rowing (coaches, Riggers, managers, retailers).

- **Support Rower**—someone who supports a rower (parent, spouse, Athletic Director) while not actually rowing.

You should notice two things here. One, there is very little separation by gender or age within the types. Rowing is a sport where gender or age do not make much of a difference—as compared to other sports, like football.

Two, there may be some crossovers between types. For example, there are some folks who are Livelihood Rowers (they coach) so they can make enough money to support their Sport Rowing efforts. But it seems that for the most part folks tend to fall into one type or the other.

A Breather

We've covered quite a bit—let's take a moment to gather our wits and recap.

For the sake of this effort, today's rowing can be divided into four different types. Within each type there may be a wide range of rowers, such as:

- disabled
- open water
- recreational
- collegiate
- masters
- youth

and on and on.

Now let me present you with this (I know, I know… I said this was going to be a breather!). Each rower will have a different level of knowledge about what they are doing. For example, a novice-Sport-Rower may actually know very little about what they are doing, whereas an elite-Sport-Rower knows quite a lot.

* * *

You are probably thinking these past few pages were a slow journey to get to a place where we can discuss improving your rowing.

You are right, it was slow—and that dear reader is how we are going to get to enjoyment (and speed if that's your gig).

Now let me ask you this: can YOU find happiness in YOUR rowing.

Let me throw an answer out here: Yes. No. It depends.

Depends on what? Four things mostly. They are:

- Why you row
- The tools you use while you row
- How successful you deal with the roadblocks of rowing
- How effectively you pay the tolls at the toll booths of rowing

Might sound overwhelming, but it's not. The rest of this workbook is about figuring out why you row. Then the next three workbooks in the series will cover:

> ➢ 10 Powerful Tools to Find Happiness from Your Rowing
> ➢ 7 Critical Rowing Roadblocks and How to Smash Through Them
> ➢ 10 Smart Ways to Overcome the Tolls of Rowing

Yes, there are other workbooks to read. However, if you only read this one looking at now, you'll be significantly further (and faster) down the river.

Okay, to the subject at hand. Let's focus on the first item which your rowing-happiness depends upon—why you row?

Mike Davenport

Why Do You Row?

It's so easy to blow off this question. You're busy, right? Lot's of things happening in your life, aren't there? Why bother?

Because if you want to find enjoyment from rowing (any activity really) and you want to find speed that might not be coming easily, you need to stop, be mindful, and answer this question.

There are two angles from which we can look at this question: Either you are **currently rowing and you are looking for happiness**. Or you are **looking for happiness and you want to know if rowing can help you find it**.

An important item to keep in mind is that the key word here is *you*. We are not interested in everyone else in the world, we are just interested in whether *YOU* can find happiness when *YOU* row.

Let's look at the first angle:

Angle #1 You Row And Are Searching For Happiness

Folks row for many different reasons. Some are trying to win the big race, or to make the national team or to compete in the Olympics. Their experience on the water is usually a real fight, pushing themselves and their abilities to the limit.

Someone else may want to experience a nice relaxed row. Just to be out with nature.

While others may want the thrilling experience of rowing miles away from shore out in the open ocean with little to remind them of landward problems.

You can get a lot of different experiences in rowing—like at *Alice's Restaurant*, you can get almost anything you want. With that said, what do you want your experience to be? In other words, **why do you row? (What experience are you searching for?)**

Rowing will definitely give you a wealth and variety of experiences. Some of those will be experiences you weren't exactly looking for. Just make sure that they are all safe and survivable experiences.

As one coach told me, "Experience surely teaches that there's a small but important difference between keeping your chin up and sticking your neck out."

So why do you row?

This simple question makes some people very nervous. Many folks I row with say they have no idea why they row. At least that's what they say up front—I don't believe them.

It's not that they are dishonest; they know why they row, but they've never spent the time to define why.

So, what about you? **Why do *you* row?**

Knowing why you row can be extremely helpful. I believe that if you don't know why you row, you won't be able to find happiness from it. Not knowing would be like going on a hike without knowing your destination, and without a destination there is little or no hope for enjoyment and happiness.

So now, let's get down to it. Why *exactly* do you row?

JOB 1: Why Do You Row?

Problem: Fairly simply, you are a rower and you're here to figure out why you do it.

Needed: Something to write with, and some peace and quiet.

You are here because in some manner or form you are involved in rowing. This means you fall into one of the categories of rowers that we listed in the previous chapter. This also means you use rowing to get to a destination. So let me ask you, **do you know what that destination is?**

If you don't know, then you've got things a little backwards—the outboard motor is before the launch, so to speak. In other words, you are going on a trip, but you don't know where you are going. So let's put things back in order and get that motor back where it belongs.

Before we go one step further let me suggest that some of you really do know why you row. If you feel confident you know exactly why you are rowing (good for you!), then pat yourself on the back (but do you *honestly* know why you are rowing?), skip to the next part of this chapter (are you *absolutely* sure?), and we'll catch up to you in a few moments (you'll be missing out if you don't stay!).

But for the rest of us, let's try to pin down why we row…

Action 1: Peace and quiet. Find some space where you can think undisturbed. You are going to have to be straightforward with yourself so limit your distractions so you can think clearly.

Action 2: Quiz. Let's take a short quiz and figure out how much you are enjoying your rowing. Flip ahead to *JOB 2: How Much Enjoyment Are You Getting From Your Rowing?*, which is the next JOB in this chapter and do Action 1. After you've done that step, write down your score and return here.

Go do that now!

Okay, you're back... Now take your number from your Pleasure Measure and write it down. What I want you to do is finish this JOB. Then redo your Pleasure Measure and see if the knowledge you get from this JOB changes your measure's reading.

Action 3: List. Now grab your piece of paper and you're going to make a list. Not just any list, mind you, but a very crucial list. On the very top of the paper, in large letters write this—

Why I Row!

Now I want you to write down the reasons why you row. Write them all down. This is no time to be judgmental, so don't—be creative here! Stop editing...write!!

Scribble down all the reasons you can muster up. A few examples are:
* I row to *meet people*
* I row to *be outside*
* I row to *make an Olympic team*
* I row to *get in shape*
* I row to *be competitive*
* I row to *see Great Blue Herons*

Whatever your reasons are, write them down. This step may take you longer, or shorter, than you think. Just keep in mind that time is not important here. Being honest with yourself is.

Action 4: Take a break. Once you've completed your list you need to get away from it. I've usually found when I write stuff like this that a minimum break of 20 minutes works best for me. This helps me clear my thoughts and I return to the project with enthusiasm and possibly a different viewpoint. So put your paper in a safe place and take a break. Go row an erg piece. I'll wait.

Action 5: List review. Return to your quiet spot and pull out your list again. Go through it with a judgmental eye. Have any additions or subtractions? Any reasons that don't make the grade? Get rid of them.

Action 6: Break again. Another short break is in order. This would be a great time for a little Ben and Jerry's, *if you know what I mean*. Just don't get ice cream all over your list.

Action 7: Prioritize. Find your space and list again. This time you're going to prioritize your reasons. Go through and number them in order of their importance to you. Be very judgmental here.

Now grab a new sheet of paper (or use the reverse side) and at the top once again write **Why I Row.** Underneath write your reasons in order.

Now take a deep breath, step back a moment, and pat yourself on the back. You've done it! You now have a list of the reason(s) why you row. These are your destinations (your point B's) that you want to reach and you are using rowing to get there.

Any revelations here?

Every time I do this JOB with rowers I usually get two types of reactions. One reaction is that I see folks' Pleasure Measure sustain an immediate jump higher.

The other type of reaction, which I don't see nearly as much, is some people stop rowing. You may be saying, "**Stop rowing. That's not good at all!**" But in some cases it is actually good.

There are some people who row for the wrong reasons and because of that they will never find happiness in it.

As much as I like to see everyone rowing, I don't want to see people row who aren't enjoying it. It is not good for them, and not good for rowing.

Action 8: Make a map. You can now consider this list of yours a map. It is going to be something you can use to help you get to your destination. Like any map it should be handy, so stow it so you can review it often and easily.

I keep my map in the left-hand drawer of my desk at work. Every day I pull it out and read it, and sometimes more than once a day. Here is my map for why I row (I mostly coach, so I classify myself a Livelihood Rower):

My Map—Why I Row

1. To teach rowers skills they need to be successful in life.

2. To build positive character traits in rowers.

3. To maintain a "safe" program.

4. To develop fast boats.

This map helps me find happiness because it keeps things in perspective. If we lose a race, it helps me remember that the win/loss record is not as important to me as the rowers learning the skills they need to be successful in life (like handling adversity). It reminds me that winning is not as important as building positive character traits in the rowers (like sportsmanship).

The map also helps me be safer. If I am having a hard time accepting the fact that wind or ice has caused us to miss a couple of practices, then I will look at my map. I realize that, if we miss a practice, it's okay. It is more important that we are safe and the rowers are learning a skill, which in this case could be how to be adaptable.

So use your map as a reminder. When you look back on what you have accomplished at a practice, or during a season, your map can show you if you are on track reaching your destination.

WARNING—One word of caution here—make sure the map you are using is your own—*DON'T USE SOMEONE ELSE'S MAP!* That's where you'll get into trouble. You don't want theirs, you want yours!

Action 9: Two more things. First, take your Pleasure Measure reading again (JOB 2, Action 1). Now compare it to the number you got from Action 2 of this JOB. Any difference?

Second, try a feel-good step—make an affirmation. An affirmation is a sentence or phrase that you repeat to yourself aloud to verbally reinforce your map.

For example, imagine for a moment that the number one reason you row is to exercise daily. A simple affirmation could be, "I row to exercise every day!"

Now imagine that you had a horrible day of rowing—like your boat rowed particularly awfully. Saying your affirmation to yourself out loud will reinforce that you reached your destination. You got out there and exercised, which is the number one reason why you row. This affirmation will help you keep the practice in perspective. But to work best affirmations need to be said out loud—mumbling doesn't cut it.

* * * * *

Now let's dig into how much enjoyment you are getting from your rowing. Seat belts buckled…air bags ready…

Mike Davenport

Do You Enjoy Rowing?

I'm not trying to trick, annoy or bum-you-out with that question. It's an important question to ask that too infrequently gets asked.

Why? No enjoyment means no return on the investment. Plain and simple.

Yeah, I know you can buy a tea pot for the stove, and you don't enjoy it, but it functions well. That's a purchase, and this is different. This is an investment of your blood, sweat, tears, energy and more. And life is too short to invest those kinds of resources, without a significant return.

So let's find out if you are enjoying your rowing, and at what level.

JOB 2: How Much Enjoyment Are You Getting From Your Rowing?

Problem: You're here because you are currently rowing and need to see how much enjoyment you're having. Or you were sent here from the previous JOB.

Needed: Something to write with and a few minutes of quiet time.

Action 1: What's your meter reading? Let's see exactly what your Pleasure Measure is currently reading. On the following list check the number that best represents your enjoyment level of rowing.

- ❒ 10—I enjoy all aspects of my rowing.
- ❒ 8—I enjoy a large amount of my rowing.
- ❒ 6—I enjoy more than 1/2 of my rowing.
- ❒ 4—I enjoy less than 1/2 of my rowing.
- ❒ 2—I enjoy a small amount of my rowing.
- ❒ 0—I can't remember the last time I enjoyed my rowing

Action 2: Meter reading of > 8. What's your reading? If you scored an eight or higher, you are definitely enjoying your rowing, and it is helping you get to a destination. If that's the case, I suggest that you zip on ahead to the next chapter.

Action 3: Meter reading of >6 but <8. Okay, not bad. But could be better.

Action 4: Meter reading of >2 but <6. Ouch, need to do some work. You might want to consider taking a slight break and re-examining why you row. Why did you get into it in the first place? And does that still matter?

- Was it social—is it filling that need?
- Was it fitness—that itch being scratched?

Try to grasp what really isn't that fun about your rowing.

Action 5: Meter reading of < 2. If your meter is showing a 2 or less then I recommend you do this next JOB.

Mike Davenport

Is Rowing Right for You?

As people we are on a never ending quest to learn, to improve, and to develop. And, of course, to seek happiness.

Rowing, in some cases, can help you with this quest. In other cases, it doesn't help.

When we "quest" we are looking for benefits, you know…stuff that makes the quest worthwhile—fame, fortune, ice cream and the such.

You may be asking, "Are there benefits I can get from rowing?" Absolutely! (And if there weren't, I would not have written this workbook, and you would not be reading it.)

You can benefit from rowing on several different planes, socially, mentally, spiritually, and physically. An immediate benefit from rowing that comes to mind is relaxation. Rowing can be a great distraction/relaxation from the day's toil—those things that take away your energy and wear you down.

Yet—I will be very straightforward here—you might not think everything in rowing is a benefit, or enjoyable. In fact there are some nasty little things that pop up every now and then, like ergometer pieces, which you might find…well…rather yucky. But those are usually short term discomforts that will payoff in long term benefits.

You are probably thinking, "Yeah, okay. That stuff sounds interesting. But I want to know if I should row or not?" Well, let's find out…

JOB 3: Is Rowing Right For You?

Problem: You have never rowed before and you need to know if you should row. Or you currently are rowing and you need to see if you have made the correct choice.

Needed: A quiet spot where you can think, twenty minutes, a pencil and sheet of paper.

When I first began rowing I had absolutely no idea what the heck was going on, or why I was doing it. I was lucky and got involved with a few nice people who took me under their wings and guided me along the way. Since then I've borrowed a system that helps me determine why I row (I go through this JOB every year and my answers do change).

Action 1: Your quiet spot. A real quiet spot where you can think without interruptions is what you are looking for. When you've found it, pull out your paper and fold it in half lengthwise. Now grab your writing stick and you're going to make two lists. The first one is…

Action 2: The good stuff. On one side of the paper make a list of all the **good things** you think you will get from rowing. As long as there is some perceived benefit to you, write it down. For example, you want to meet people—this is one of *your* good things—so write it down. And remember these are your benefits, *your* good stuff—not someone else's. Now is the time to be selfish.

One little hint—there is plenty more good stuff to be had in rowing than just winning a race. I am not the only one to think so.

Steve Fairbairn, a very famous English rowing coach, once observed, "One does not need to win a race to get enjoyment." Thank you Steve.

Action 3: The bad stuff. On the other side of the paper write down the bad stuff. What you're looking for are the hassles, distractions, or problems with rowing. Examples would be getting up early in the morning, a long drive, expensive club dues. Again these are *your* hassles and distractions—not someone else's.

Action 4: Compare notes. When you're done writing, lay the paper flat and compare the *good stuff* column to the *bad stuff* column. Read through both columns (aloud) and make sure you aren't holding back. You need to be honest with yourself here—very honest!

Now put the paper down and take a breather. Give yourself a little reward—stretch your legs, sing a song, pat the dog, feed the cat. Or yourself.

When you feel refreshed sit back down and pick up your list again. Once you are sure you have everything written down, go through and prioritize the items in each list. Number them in order of importance.

Once that is done, here comes the hard—but oh-so-important—part…

Action 5: Balance the list. Start crossing off any items on both sides of the lists that are equal. If one of your Good Stuffers is, "You get to be on the water" but a Bad Stuffer is, "You are afraid of the open spaces," then these would cancel each other out.

Action 6: What's left? When your balancing act is over, hopefully you have a good stuff column with one, or several items, that have not been canceled by anything in the bad stuff column. These items point to why you want to row. Now take these items in hand, or in mind, and give rowing a chance.

But what if you don't have anything left in your good stuff column after your balancing act (or you have a bunch of bad stuff left over)?

If you've been very honest with yourself and have done your job properly, you may have to face the fact that rowing might not be for you, and you are forecasting that there won't be any enjoyment and happiness ahead. But before you give up on rowing consider that you might not know enough about it to do your good stuff column justice.

If that might be the case, and there's doubt that you don't know enough about rowing, then gather some info. See if you can go to a rowing practice and watch. Ask a coach, if there is one, if you can ride in the chase-launch, or take a novice rowing class. Talk to some rowers, hang out in a boathouse, take a few strokes. Get as much info from as many sources as possible and then try your lists again.

Action 7: In practice. If you have moved past your list and are actually rowing, here are a few criteria that may help you determine if rowing is right for you. When a rowing event is over, whether it is a practice or a race, did you have any of these:

- A fulfillment of your motive for rowing?
- A feeling of fun?
- A lower level of anxiety or stress?
- A greater perceived competence and control level?
- A higher level of self-esteem?
- A few laughs?

Those are just a few rewards you can expect. If none are happening, or other benefits, then chances are rowing is not right for you. And here's one thing about rowing…

Now Go Slow

If you've read this workbook because you are looking for more from your rowing, then your next step is to take some of the actions I presented and actually act on them.

If you are struggling to find speed, slow down, and figure out why.

If you are thriving in your rowing and want more…slow down…pause…reflect…plan.

And keep reading.

You may want to consider getting and reading the other workbooks that go along in this series. They cover specifically how to go slower (and in turn fast) such as:

➢ *More Rowing Slow: 10 Powerful Tools to Find Happiness from Your Rowing* (Fall 2019)

➢ *Even More Rowing Slow: 7 Critical Rowing Roadblocks and How to Smash Through Them* (Winter 2020)

➢ *Stop Rowing Slow:10 Smart Ways to Overcome the Tolls of Rowing* (Spring 2020)

If you are reading this workbook and really haven't gotten into rowing yet, I suggest you find the nearest program and begin. USRowing.org can help you find the program closest you.

In a world that is moving so fast, I want to thank you for slowing yourself down to read this workbook.

Thanks for being here!

Mike Davenport
MaxRigging.com

Art by Peter Martin

- Rowing Workbooks -

✦ *Buy It Right: 8 Steps to Buy the Rowing Equipment You Need At a Price You Can Afford* (rowing workbook #1)

✦ *Get Ready Now: 12 Immediate Actions to Take Before Your Next Rowing Season* (rowing workbook #2)

✦ *Make It Last Forever: 13 Steps to Help Your Rowing Equipment Last an Eternity* (rowing workbook #3)

✦ *Nuts and Bolts Guide to Rigging: One Hundred and Fifty Steps to help you get the most from the rigging of your rowing equipment*

- Coaching workbooks -

✦ *The 3 Sinister Truths of Coaching Sports Today: And What You Can Do About Them* (coaching workbook #1)

✦ *Build Your Team: How to Create, Develop and Lead The Team of Your Dreams* (coaching workbook #2) _____

(all these books can be found at Amazon)

Printed in Great Britain
by Amazon